Sing 'n Learn
CHINESE
唱歌學中文
SECOND EDITION

Introduce Chinese with Favorite Children's Songs

By Trio Jan Jeng and Selina Yoon

MASTER
COMMUNICATIONS

Published by Master Communications, Cincinnati, Ohio U.S.A.
http://www.master-comm.com

Library of Congress Catalog Card Number: 00-91769
ISBN 1-888194-06-5 (Book & Cassette)
ISBN 1-888194-17-0 (Book & CD)
Printed in the United States of America.

Introduction

Chinese belongs to the family of Sino-Tibetan languages. It is the world's second largest family of languages (after the Indo-European family), and is made up of 300 languages that are used over a vast geographic area. These languages share a number of common features such as monosyllabism and tonality. Chinese is spoken by a quarter of the world's population, making it the most widely used language in the world. It is a very ancient language, predating English, and other European languages. Within China, there is a diversity of languages; many different ethnic groups use different languages. There are also many different dialects with widely different levels of mutual intelligiblity, such as Cantonese. **Mandarin Chinese** is the most widely used form of the Chinese language, and is also the official standard language in China. **Sing 'n Learn Chinese** uses the standard Mandarin Chinese as well.

There are 400 basic syllables formed by 21 initials and 35 finals in Chinese. A syllable is made up of three parts; an initial, a final and a tone. There are 4 tones in standard Chinese; the first tone is a high level, the second tone is a high rising, the third is a low dipping and the fourth is a high falling. The meaning of word will be altered with its tonal inflection. Chinese relies on tones and contexts to differentiate meanings. Therefore, accuracy of the tonal pronunciation of the words is crucial to the correct meaning and understanding of Chinese.

Chinese uses a system of writing in characters. A different character exists for each word. This system developed out of pictograms, in which a picture stood for a thing or object, such as a man, woman, mountain, ect. Over time, the pictograms were simplified and formalized into a system of writing, through which words are represented by characters. The appearance of Chinese characters was standardized during the Wei and Jin Dynasties (221 AD-580 AD). Currently, there are two systems of Chinese characters in use: the traditional and simplified characters. **Simplified characters** are used in modern mainland China, while **traditional characters** are used in Taiwan and Hong Kong, and by other overseas Chinese. Simplified Chinese characters were put into widespread use by the Chinese government to standardize the simplified forms that were already in use, and also to combat illiteracy, which historically has been fostered by the complexity and intricacy of the traditional characters.

Hanyu Pinyin is the Romanized Chinese Phonetic System, which is the official romanization of mainland China. In Sing 'n Learn Chinese, each line of lyric is represented by a simplified character, a traditional character and a Pinyin pronunciation. We have included both sets of characters so that you and your child may become familiar with each one.

Sing 'n Learn Chinese is the result of in-depth research and a collection of favorite children's songs sung in China and the West which are designed to teach standard spoken Chinese (Mandarin) the fun way. The songs found in **Sing 'n Learn** are authentic popular Chinese children's songs from China. The Chinese song "Two Tigers", which is one of the most popular songs in China and Taiwan, is sung to the very familiar "Frere Jacques", or "Are You Sleeping" tune in the West. Many Chinese are surprised to learn that the same tune is sung in other countries. Children and adults can enjoy these singable and danceable songs, while learning basic Chinese words and characters.

Listen to the songs often to improve your listening comprehension and pronunciation. Follow the lyrics and then sing along. You can add motions and variations to the songs for countless hours of fun learning. Background notes and activity guides are at the end of the book. We hope that you enjoy singing and learning along with our fun illustrations and music.

Four Tones

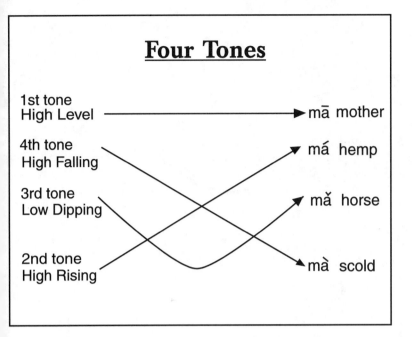

1st tone
High Level ——————————→ mā mother

4th tone
High Falling → má hemp

3rd tone
Low Dipping → mǎ horse

2nd tone
High Rising → mà scold

Guide to Pinyin Pronunciation

Pinyin	English Pronunciation
a	ah as in w**a**sh
e	e as in **e**gg
o	o as in m**o**re
u	oo as in b**oo**t
ei	a as in l**a**ke
ai	i as in b**i**te
ou	o as in l**ow**
i	e as in m**ee**t
ü	ew as in l**ew**d
q	ch in **ch**eat
x	sh in **sh**eet
z	ds in ree**ds**
c	ts in do**ts**
s	s in **s**and
zh	dg in ju**dg**e
ch	ch in **ch**ildren
sh	sh in **sh**eaf

CHINESE PRONUNCIATION TABLE

Vowels / Consonants	b	p	m	f	d	t	n	l	z	c	s	zh	ch	sh	r	j	q	x	g	k	h
a (a, ai, ao, an, ang)	ba bai bao ban bang	pa pai pao pan pang	ma mai mao man mang	fa fan fang	da dai dao dan dang	ta tai tao tan tang	na nai nao nan nang	la lai lao lan lang	za zai zao zan zang	ca cai cao can cang	sa sai sao san sang	zha zhai zhao zhan zhang	cha chai chao chan chang	sha shai shao shan shang	rao ran rang				ga gai gao gan gang	ka kai kao kan kang	ha hai hao han hang
o (o, ong, ou)	bo	po pou	mo mou	fou	dong dou	tong tou	nong nou	long lou	zong zou	cong cou	song sou	zhong zhou	chong chou	shou	rong rou				gong gou	kong kou	hong hou
e (e, ei, en, eng, er)	bei ben beng	pei pen peng	mei men meng	fei fen feng	de den deng	te teng	ne nei nen neng	le lei leng	ze zei zen zeng	ce cen ceng	se sen seng	zhe zhei zhen zheng	che chen cheng	she shei shen sheng	re ren reng				ge gei gen geng	ke gei gen geng	ge gei gen geng
i (i, ia, iao, ie, iu, ian, iang, in, ing, iong)	bi bie bian bin bing	pi piao pie pian pin ping	mi miao mie miu mian min ming		di diao die diu dian ding	ti tiao tie tiu tian tiang tin ting tiong	ni niao nie niu nian niang nin ning niong	li lia liao lie liu lian liang lin ling liong	zi	ci	si	zhi	chi	shi	ri	ji jia jiao jie jiu jian jiang jin jing jiong	qi qia qiao qie qiu qian qiang qin qing qiong	xi xia xiao xie xiu xian xiang xin xing xiong			
u (u, ua, uo, ui, uai, uan, un, uang, ueng)	bu	pu	mu	fu	du duo dui duan dun	tu tuo tui tuan tun	nu nuo nuan	lu luo lui luan lun	zu zuo zui zuan zun	cu cuo cui cuan cun	su suo sui suan sun	zhu zhua zhuo zhui zhuan zhun zhuang	chu chua chuo chui chuai chuan chun chuang	shu shua shuo shui shuai shuan shun shuang	ru rua ruo rui ruan run				gu gua guo gui guai guan gun guang	ku kua kuo kui kuai kuan kun kuang	hu hua huo hui huai huan hun huang
ü (ü, üe, üan, ün)					nü nüe	lü lüe										jü jüe jüan jün	qü qüe qüan qün	xü xüe xüan xün			

你　好
你　好
Nǐ　Hǎo

你　好，你　好，
你　好，你　好，
Nǐ　hǎo,　nǐ　hǎo,

我　很　好，我　很　好。
我　很　好，我　很　好。
Wǒ　hén　hǎo,　wǒ　hén　hǎo.

我　们　一　起　唱　歌，
我　們　一　起　唱　歌，
Wǒ　mén　yì　qǐ　chàng gē,

我　们　一　起　唱　歌，
我　們　一　起　唱　歌，
Wǒ　mén　yì　qǐ　chàng gē,

真　快　乐，真　快　乐。
眞　快　樂，眞　快　樂。
Zhēn kuài lè,　Zhēn kuài lè

How are You?

How are you?
How are you?
I am fine.
I am fine.
Let's sing together,
Let's sing together.
How happy we are,
How happy we are!

米　米
汤　汤
Tāng mǐ

Tommy Panda

尼　尼
潘　潘
Pān ní

Penny Panda

4

十　个　小　朋　友
十　個　小　朋　友
Shí　gè　xiǎo　péng　yǒu

一　个　，两　个　，三　个　小　朋　友，
一　個　，兩　個　，三　個　小　朋　友，
Yí　gè,　liǎng　gè,　sān　gè　xiǎo　péng　yǒu,

四　个　，五　个　，六　个　小　朋　友，
四　個　，五　個　，六　個　小　朋　友，
Sì　gè,　wǔ　gè,　liù　gè　xiǎo　péng　yǒu,

七　个　，八　个　，九　个　小　朋　友，
七　個　，八　個　，九　個　小　朋　友，
Qī　gè,　bā　gè,　jiǔ　gè　xiǎo　péng　yǒu,

十　个　小　朋　友。
十　個　小　朋　友。
Shí　gè　xiǎo　péng　yǒu.

Ten Little Friends

One, two, three little friends
Four, five, six little friends
Seven, eight, nine little friends
Ten little friends.

我 们 这 样 来 洗 脸
我 們 這 樣 來 洗 臉
Wǒ mén zhè yàng lái xǐ liǎn

我 们 这 样 来 洗 脸，
我 們 這 樣 來 洗 臉，
Wǒ mén zhè yàng lái xǐ liǎn,

来 洗 脸，来 洗 脸，
來 洗 臉，來 洗 臉，
lái xǐ liǎn, lái xǐ liǎn,

我 们 这 样 来 洗 脸，
我 們 這 樣 來 洗 臉，
Wǒ mén zhè yàng lái xǐ liǎn,

一 大 清 早。
一 大 清 早。
yí dà qīng zǎo.

洗 脸
洗 臉
xǐ liǎn

刷 牙
刷 牙
shuā yá

我 们 这 样 来 刷 牙，
我 們 這 樣 來 刷 牙，
Wǒ mén zhè yàng lái shuā yá,

来 刷 牙，来 刷 牙，
來 刷 牙，來 刷 牙，
lái shuā yá, lái shuā yá,

我 们 这 样 来 刷 牙，
我 們 這 樣 來 刷 牙，
Wǒ mén zhè yàng lái shuā yá,

一 大 清 早。
一 大 清 早。
yí dà qīng zǎo.

This is the Way We Wash Our Face

This is the way we wash our face,
wash our face, wash our face,
This is the way we wash our face,
early in the morning.

This is the way we brush our teeth,
brush our teeth, brush our teeth,
This is the way we brush our teeth,
early in the morning.

梳梳头头
shū tóu

我们这样来梳头，
我們這樣來梳頭，
Wǒ mén zhè yàng lái shū tóu,

来梳头，来梳头，
來梳頭，來梳頭，
lái shū tóu, lái shū tóu,

我们这样来梳头，
我們這樣來梳頭，
Wǒ mén zhè yàng lái shū tóu,

一大清早。
一大清早。
yí dà qīng zǎo.

我们这样来穿衣服，
我們這樣來穿衣服，
Wǒ mén zhè yàng lái chuān yī fú,

来穿衣服，来穿衣服，
來穿衣服，來穿衣服
lái chuān yī fú, lái chuān yī fú,

我们这样来穿衣服，
我們這樣來穿衣服，
Wǒ mén zhè yàng lái chuān yī fú,

一大清早。
一大清早。
yí dà qīng zǎo.

穿衣服
穿衣服
chuān yī fú

This is the way we comb our hair,
comb our hair, comb our hair,
This is the way we comb our hair,
early in the morning.

This is the way we put on our dress,
put on our dress, put on our dress,
This is the way we put on our dress,
early in the morning.

当　我　们　同　在　一　起
當　我　們　同　在　一　起
Dāng　wǒ　mén　tóng　zài　yì　qǐ

When We Are Together

当　我　们　同　在　一　起，在　一　起，在　一　起，
當　我　們　同　在　一　起，在　一　起，在　一　起，
Dāng　wǒ　mén　tóng　zài　yì　qǐ，　zài　yì　qǐ，　zài　yì　qǐ，

当　我　们　同　在　一　起，其　快　乐　无　比。
當　我　們　同　在　一　起，其　快　樂　無　比。
Dāng　wǒ　mén　tóng　zài　yì　qǐ，　qí　kuài　lè　wú　bǐ.

你　对　着　我　笑　嘻　嘻，我　对　着　你　笑　哈　哈，
你　對　著　我　笑　嘻　嘻，我　對　著　你　笑　哈　哈，
Nǐ　dùi　zhè　wǒ　xiào　xī　xī，　wǒ　dùi　zhè　nǐ　xiào　hā　hā,

当　我　们　同　在　一　起，其　快　乐　无　比。
當　我　們　同　在　一　起，其　快　樂　無　比。
Dāng　wǒ　mén　tóng　zài　yì　qǐ，　qí　kuài　lè　wú　bǐ.

When we are
Together, together, together
When we are together,
we are happy as can be.
You look at me, I look at you,
we smiled at each other.
When we are together,
we are happy as can be.

When my father and I are
Together, together, together
When my father and I are together,
we are happy as can be.
Father looks at me, I look at him,
we smiled at each other.
When my father and I are together,
we are happy as can be.

我 和 爸 爸 同 在 一 起 ，在 一 起 ，在 一 起 ，
我 和 爸 爸 同 在 一 起 ，在 一 起 ，在 一 起 ，
Wǒ hé bà bà tóng zài yì qǐ, zài yì qǐ, zài yì qǐ,

我 和 爸 爸 同 在 一 起 ，其 快 乐 无 比 。
我 和 爸 爸 同 在 一 起 ，其 快 樂 無 比 。
Wǒ hé bà bà tóng zài yì qǐ, qí kuài lè wú bǐ.

你 对 着 我 笑 嘻 嘻 ，我 对 着 你 笑 哈 哈 ，
你 對 著 我 笑 嘻 嘻 ，我 對 著 你 笑 哈 哈 ，
Nǐ dùi zhe wǒ xiào xī xī, wǒ dùi zhe nǐ xiào hā hā,

我 和 爸 爸 同 在 一 起 ，其 快 乐 无 比 。
我 和 爸 爸 同 在 一 起 ，其 快 樂 無 比 。
Wǒ hé bà bà tóng zài yì qǐ, qí kuài lè wú bǐ.

如 果 你 很 高 兴
如 果 你 很 高 興
Rú guǒ nǐ hěn gāo xìng

拍 拍 手
拍 拍 手
pāi pai shǒu

（一）
如 果 你 很 高 兴，你 拍 拍 手。
如 果 你 很 高 興，你 拍 拍 手。
Rú guǒ nǐ hěn gāo xìng, nǐ pāi pai shǒu.

如 果 你 很 高 兴，你 拍 拍 手。
如 果 你 很 高 興，你 拍 拍 手。
Rú guǒ nǐ hěn gāo xìng, nǐ pāi pai shǒu.

如 果 你 很 高 兴，你 一 定 会 笑 哈 哈。
如 果 你 很 高 興，你 一 定 會 笑 哈 哈。
Rú guǒ nǐ hěn gāo xìng, nǐ yí dìng hùi xiao hā hā.

如 果 你 很 高 兴，你 拍 拍 手。
如 果 你 很 高 興，你 拍 拍 手。
Rú guǒ nǐ hěn gāo xìng, nǐ pāi pai shǒu.

If You are Happy

(1)
If you are happy, clap your hands (clap clap)
If you are happy, clap your hands (clap clap)
If you are happy, you will be sure to laugh, ha ha.

(2)
If you are happy, stomp your feet, (stomp stomp)
If you are happy, stomp your feet, (stomp stomp)
If you are happy, you will be sure to laugh, ha ha.

(3)
If you are happy, shout hooray, (hooray)
If you are happy, shout hooray, (hooray)
If you are happy, you will be sure to laugh, ha ha.

(4)
If you are happy, do all three, (clap clap, stomp stomp, hooray)
If you are happy, do all three, (clap clap, stomp stomp, hooray)
If you are happy, you will be sure to laugh, ha ha.

（二）
如 果 你 很 高 兴，你 踏 踏 脚。
如 果 你 很 高 興，你 踏 踏 腳。
Rú guǒ nǐ hěn gāo xìng, nǐ tà tà jiǎo.

如 果 你 很 高 兴，你 踏 踏 脚。
如 果 你 很 高 興，你 踏 踏 腳。
Rú guǒ nǐ hěn gāo xìng, nǐ tà tà jiǎo.

如 果 你 很 高 兴，你 一 定 会 笑 哈 哈。
如 果 你 很 高 興，你 一 定 會 笑 哈 哈。
Rú guǒ nǐ hěn gāo xìng, nǐ yí dìng hùi xiào hā hā.

如 果 你 很 高 兴，你 踏 踏 脚。
如 果 你 很 高 興，你 踏 踏 腳。
Rú guǒ nǐ hěn gāo xìng, nǐ tà tà jiǎo.

万 岁
萬 歲
wàn suì

（三）
你 大 声 喊（万 岁）。
你 大 聲 喊（萬 歲）。
Nǐ dà shēng hǎn (wàn suì).

（四）
你 做 全 部（拍 手、踏 脚、万 岁）。
你 做 全 部（拍 手、踏 腳、萬 岁）。
Nǐ zuò quán bù (pāi shǒu, tà jiǎo, wàn suì).

踏 踏 脚
踏 踏 腳
tà tà jiǎo

11

蜜蜂工作
蜜蜂工作
Mì fēng gōng zuò

嗡 嗡 嗡，嗡 嗡 嗡，大 家 一 起 勤 做 工，
嗡 嗡 嗡，嗡 嗡 嗡，大 家 一 起 勤 做 工，
Wēng wēng wēng, wēng wēng wēng, dà jiā yì qǐ qín zuò gōng,

来 匆 匆，去 匆 匆，做 工 兴 味 浓。
來 匆 匆，去 匆 匆，做 工 興 味 濃。
Lái cōng cōng, qù cōng cōng, zuò gōng xìng wèi nóng.

天 暖 花 好 不 做 工，将 来 那 里 好 过 冬，
天 暖 花 好 不 做 工，將 來 那 裡 好 過 冬，
Tiān nuǎn huā hǎo bú zuò gōng, jiāng lái nǎ lǐ hǎo guò dōng,

嗡 嗡 嗡，嗡 嗡 嗡，别 学 懒 惰 虫。
嗡 嗡 嗡，嗡 嗡 嗡，別 學 懶 惰 蟲。
Wēng wēng wēng, wēng wēng wēng, bié xué lǎn duò chóng.

Working Bees

Buzz buzz buzz, buzz buzz buzz,
Let us work together. Let us hurry up,
Let's hurry up, we love to work.
If we don't work hard while the flowers bloom,
The winter will be hard.
Buzz buzz buzz, buzz buzz buzz,
Don't be a lazy bug.

伦 敦 大 桥
倫 敦 大 橋
Lún　Dūn　Dà　qiáo

伦 敦 大 桥 垮 下 来 ，垮 下 来 ，垮 下 来 ，
倫 敦 大 橋 垮 下 來 ，垮 下 來 ，垮 下 來 ，
Lún dūn dà qiáo kuǎ xià lái, kuǎ xià lái, kuǎ xià lái,

伦 敦 大 桥 垮 下 来 ，就 要 垮 下 来 。
倫 敦 大 橋 垮 下 來 ，就 要 垮 下 來 。
Lún dūn dà qiáo kuǎ xià lái, jiù yào kuǎ xià lái.

London Bridge

London big bridge is falling down,
Falling down, falling down.
London big bridge is falling down.
It is falling down.

唱 歌 跳 舞
唱 歌 跳 舞
Chàng gē tiào wǔ

(一)
把 右 手 放 裡 面，
把 右 手 放 裡 面，
Bǎ yòu shǒu fàng lǐ mìan,

把 右 手 放 外 面，
把 右 手 放 外 面，
Bǎ yòu shǒu fàng wài mìan,

把 右 手 放 裡 面，
把 右 手 放 裡 面，
Bǎ yòu shǒu fàng lǐ mìan,

搖 搖 你 的 手，唱 歌 跳 舞，
搖 搖 你 的 手，唱 歌 跳 舞，
Yáo yáo nǐ dè shǒu, chàng gē tiào wǔ,

轉 個 圓 圈，大 家 笑 哈 哈。
轉 個 圓 圈，大 家 笑 哈 哈。
Zhuàn gē yuán quān, dà jiā xiào hā hā.

(二) 左 手 搖 搖 你 的 手
左 手 搖 搖 你 的 手
Zuǒ shǒu yáo yáo nǐ dè shǒu

(三) 右 腳 搖 搖 你 的 腳
右 腳 搖 搖 你 的 腳
Yòu jiǎo yáo yáo nǐ dè jiǎo

(四) 左 腳 搖 搖 你 的 腳
左 腳 搖 搖 你 的 腳
Zuǒ jiǎo yáo yáo nǐ dè jiǎo

(五) 自 己 搖 搖 你 自 己
自 己 搖 搖 你 自 己
Zì jǐ yáo yáo nǐ zì jǐ

Sing Songs & Dance

Put your right hand in,
Put your right hand out,
Put your right hand in, and shake your hand,
Sing a song, and dance, turn around
Everybody laugh.

2. left hand
3. right foot
4. left foot
5. whole self in

14

膝膝
xī

膀膀
肩肩
jiān bǎng

头頭
Tóu

脚腳
jiǎo

头 儿 ， 肩 膀 ， 膝 和 脚
頭 兒 ， 肩 膀 ， 膝 和 腳
Tóu ér, jiān bǎng, xī hé jiǎo

头 儿 ， 肩 膀 ， 膝 和 脚 ， 膝 和 脚 ，
頭 兒 ， 肩 膀 ， 膝 和 腳 ， 膝 和 腳 ，
Tóu ér, jiān bǎng, xī hé jiǎo, xī hé jiǎo

头 儿 ， 肩 膀 ， 膝 和 脚 ， 膝 和 脚 ，
頭 兒 ， 肩 膀 ， 膝 和 腳 ， 膝 和 腳 ，
Tóu ér, jiān bǎng, xī hé jiǎo, xī hé jiǎo,

眼 ， 耳 ， 口 和 鼻 ，
眼 ， 耳 ， 口 和 鼻 ，
Yǎn, ěr, kǒu hé bí,

头 儿 ， 肩 膀 ， 膝 和 脚 ， 膝 和 脚 。
頭 兒 ， 肩 膀 ， 膝 和 腳 ， 膝 和 腳 。
Tóu ér, jiān bǎng, xī hé jiǎo, xī hé jiǎo

Head, Shoulders, Knees & Feet

Head, shoulders, knees and feet, knees and feet
Head, shoulders, knees and feet, knees and feet
Eyes, ears, mouth and nose
Head, shoulders, knees and feet, knees and feet.

眼眼
Yǎn

耳耳
ěr

口口
kǒu

鼻鼻
bí

朵朵
耳耳
Ěr duo

睛晴
眼眼
yǎn jīng

子子
鼻鼻
bí zi

個
兩
朵
耳
个 两 朵 耳
個 兩 朵 耳
gè liǎng duo Ěr

手手 指指 头頭
shǒu zhǐ tóu

耳耳 朵朵 两两 个個，眼眼 睛晴 两两 个個，鼻鼻 子子 一一 个個，
Ěr duo liǎng gè， yǎn jīng liǎng gè， bí zi yī gè，

嘴嘴 巴巴 有有 一一 个個，头頭 有有 一一 个個，手手 有有 两两 个個，
Zuǐ bā yǒu yī gè， tóu yǒu yī gè， shǒu yǒu liǎng gè．

脚脚 有有 两两 个個，手手 指指 头頭 十十 个個，
Jiǎo yǒu liǎng gè， shǒu zhǐ tóu shí gè，

啦啦 ·······················
啦啦 ·······················
Lā ·······················

Two Ears

Two ears, two eyes, one nose
One mouth, one head, two hands,
Two feet, ten fingers
La la la la la la la la la la ....

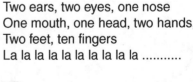

嘴嘴 巴巴
Zuǐ bā

脚脚
Jiǎo

手手
shǒu

头頭
tóu

17

妹 妹 有 只 小 绵 羊
妹 妹 有 隻 小 綿 羊
Mèi mèi yǒu zhī xiǎo mián yáng

妹 妹 有 只 小 绵 羊，小 绵 羊，小 绵 羊，
妹 妹 有 隻 小 綿 羊，小 綿 羊，小 綿 羊，
Mèi mèi yǒu zhī xiǎo mián yáng, xiǎo mián yáng, xiǎo mián yáng,

妹 妹 有 只 小 绵 羊，羊 毛 白 雪 亮。
妹 妹 有 隻 小 綿 羊，羊 毛 白 雪 亮。
Mèi mèi yǒu zhī xiǎo mián yáng, yáng máo bái xuě liàng.

不 论 妹 妹 去 哪 里，去 哪 里，去 哪 里，
不 論 妹 妹 去 哪 裡，去 哪 裡，去 哪 裡，
Bú lùn mèi mèi qù nǎ lǐ, qù nǎ lǐ, qù nǎ lǐ,

不 论 妹 妹 去 哪 里，小 绵 羊 也 去。
不 論 妹 妹 去 哪 裡，小 綿 羊 也 去。
Bú lùn mèi mèi qù nǎ lǐ, xiǎo mián yáng yě qù.

Little Sister had a Little Lamb

Little sister had a little lamb, little lamb, little lamb,
Little sister had a little lamb,
Whose fleece was bright as white snow.
No matter where sister went, sister went, sister went
No matter where sister went, the lamb was sure to go.

找　朋　友
找　朋　友
Zhǎo péng yǒu

一 二 三 四 五 六 七，
一 二 三 四 五 六 七，
Yī èr sān sì wǔ liù qī,

我 的 朋 友 在 哪 里，
我 的 朋 友 在 哪 裡，
Wǒ dē péng yǒu zài nǎ lǐ,

在 这 里，在 这 里，
在 這 裡，在 這 裡，
Zài zhè lǐ, zài zhè lǐ,

我 的 朋 友 在 这 里。
我 的 朋 友 在 這 裡。
Wǒ dē péng yǒu zài zhè lǐ.

（二） （三） （四）
妈 妈　哥 哥　姐 姐
媽 媽　哥 哥　姊 姊
Mā ma　Gē ge　Jiě jie

Where is My Friend ?

One, two, three, four, five, six, seven
Where is my friend?
Here he is, here he is.
Here is my friend.

2. Where is my mother?
3. Where is my older brother?
4. Where is my older sister?

一　二　三　四　五　六　七　八　九　十
yī, èr, sān, sì, wǔ, liù, qī, bā, jiǔ, shí
1　2　3　4　5　6　7　8　9　10

19

花 园 里 的 洋 娃 娃
花 園 裡 的 洋 娃 娃
Huā yuán lǐ dè yáng wá wa

妹 妹 背 著 洋 娃 娃 ， 走 到 花 园 来 看 花 ，
妹 妹 背 著 洋 娃 娃 ， 走 到 花 園 來 看 花 ，
Mèi mei bēi zhè yáng wá wa, zǒu dào huā yuán lái kàn huā,

娃 娃 饿 了 叫 妈 妈 ， 树 上 小 鸟 笑 哈 哈 。
娃 娃 餓 了 叫 媽 媽 ， 樹 上 小 鳥 笑 哈 哈 。
Wá wa è lè jiào mā ma, shù shàng xiǎo niǎo xiào hā hā.

Doll in the Garden

Little girl was carrying the baby doll
To see the flowers in the garden.
The baby doll was hungry and called out for mommy
The bird on the tree laughed, ha ha.

什 么 颜 色
什 麼 顏 色
Shén mò yán sè

红 色，红 色，谁 穿 红 衣 服？
紅 色，紅 色，誰 穿 紅 衣 服？
Hóng sè, hóng sè, shuí chuān hóng yī fú?

汤 米，汤 米，汤 米，汤 米，
湯 米，湯 米，湯 米，湯 米，
Tāng mǐ, tāng mǐ, tāng mǐ, tāng mǐ

穿 红 衣 服。
穿 紅 衣 服。
Chuān hóng yí fú.

紫 色，紫 色，谁 穿 紫 衣 服？
紫 色，紫 色，誰 穿 紫 衣 服？
Zǐ sè, zǐ sè, shuí chuān zǐ yī fú?

潘 尼，潘 尼，潘 尼，潘 尼，
潘 尼，潘 尼，潘 尼，潘 尼，
Pān ní, Pān ní, Pān ní, Pān ní

穿 紫 衣 服。
穿 紫 衣 服。
Chuān zǐ yī fú.

What Color?

Red, Red, Who's wearing red?
Tommy, Tommy, Tommy, Tommy
Wears red clothes.
Purple, Purple, Who's wearing purple?
Penny, Penny, Penny, Penny
Wears purple clothes.

王 老 先 生 有 块 地
王 老 先 生 有 塊 地
Wáng lǎo xiān shēng yǒu kuài dì

（一）
王 老 先 生 有 块 地，依 呀 依 呀 哟。
王 老 先 生 有 塊 地，依 呀 依 呀 喲。
Wáng lǎo xiān shēng yǒu kuài dì, yī yā yī yā yōu.

他 在 田 里 养 小 鸡，依 呀 依 呀 哟。
他 在 田 裡 養 小 雞，依 呀 依 呀 喲。
Tā zài tián lǐ yǎng xiǎo jī, yī yā yī yā yōu.

吱 吱 吱，吱 吱 吱，
吱 吱 吱，吱 吱 吱，
Zhī zhī zhī, Zhī zhī zhī,

吱 吱 吱，吱 吱 吱，吱 吱 吱，
吱 吱 吱，吱 吱 吱，吱 吱 吱，
Zhī zhī zhī, Zhī zhī zhī, Zhī zhī zhī,

王 老 先 生 有 块 地，依 呀 依 呀 哟。
王 老 先 生 有 塊 地，依 呀 依 呀 喲。
Wáng lǎo xiān shēng yǒu kuài dì, yī yā yī yā yōu.

（二）小 狗，汪 汪 汪
　　　小 狗，汪 汪 汪
　　　Xiǎo gǒu, Wāng wāng wāng

（三）小 猫，喵 喵 喵
　　　小 貓，喵 喵 喵
　　　Xiǎo māo, Miāo miāo miāo

（四）小 猪，公 公 公
　　　小 豬，公 公 公
　　　Xiǎo zhū, Gōng gōng gōng

Old Mr. Wong had a Farm Field

Old Mr. Wong has a farm field, I EI I EI O
He raises little chicken in the field, I EI I EI O
zhi zhi zhi zhi zhi zhi zhi zhi zhi zhi zhi zhi
Old Mr. Wong has a farm field, I EI I EI O

2) Dog — wong wong wong wong
3) Cat — miao miao miao miao miao miao
4) Pig — gong gong gong gong gong

24

五　只　小　鴨　出　去　玩
五　隻　小　鴨　出　去　玩
Wǔ　zhī　xiǎo　yā　chū　qù　wán

五　只　小　鴨　出　去　玩，
五　隻　小　鴨　出　去　玩，
Wǔ　zhī　xiǎo　yā　chū　qù　wán,

经　过　了　高　山　到　很　远，
經　過　了　高　山　到　很　遠，
jīng　guò　le　gāo　shān　dào　hén　yuǎn,

鴨　子　妈　妈　呱　呱　叫，四　只　小　鴨　跑　回　来。
鴨　子　媽　媽　呱　呱　叫，四　隻　小　鴨　跑　回　来。
Yā　zǐ　mā　mā　guā　guā　jiào. sì　zhī　xiǎo　yā　pǎo　húi　lái.

四　只　小　鴨　出　去　玩，…三　只　小　鴨　跑　回　来。
四　隻　小　鴨　出　去　玩，…三　隻　小　鴨　跑　回　來。
Sì　zhī　xiǎo　yā　chū　qù　wán,　sān　zhī　xiǎo　yā　pǎo　húi　lái.

三　只　小　鴨　出　去　玩，…两　只　小　鴨　跑　回　来。
三　隻　小　鴨　出　去　玩，…兩　隻　小　鴨　跑　回　來。
Sān　zhī　xiǎo　yā　chū　qù　wán,　liǎng zhī　xiǎo　yā　pǎo　húi　lái.

两　只　小　鴨　出　去　玩，…一　只　小　鴨　跑　回　来。
兩　隻　小　鴨　出　去　玩，…一　隻　小　鴨　跑　回　來。
Liǎng　zhī　xiǎo　yā　chū　qù　wán,　yì　zhī　xiǎo　yā　pǎo　húi　lái.

一　只　小　鴨　出　去　玩，…没　有　小　鴨　跑　回　来。
一　隻　小　鴨　出　去　玩，…没　有　小　鴨　跑　回　來。
Yì　zhī　xiǎo　yā　chū　qù　wán,　méi　yǒu　xiǎo　yā　pǎo　húi　lái.

然　后　鴨　子　妈　妈　到　处　找，
然　後　鴨　子　媽　媽　到　處　找，
Rán　hòu　yā　zǐ　mā　mā　dào　chù　zhǎo,

鴨　子　妈　妈　大　声　叫：呱、呱、呱。
鴨　子　媽　媽　大　聲　叫：呱、呱、呱。
Yā　zǐ　mā　mā　dà　shēng　jiào : guā,　guā,　guā.

五　只　小　鴨　跑　回　来。
五　隻　小　鴨　跑　回　來。
Wǔ　zhī　xiǎo　yā　pǎo　húi　lái.

Five Little Ducks

Five little ducks went out to play
Over the hills and far away
Mommy duck said quack quack quack.
Four little ducks came running back.

Four little ducks went out to play
Over the hills and far away
Mommy duck said quack quack quack.
Three little ducks came running back.

Three little ducks went out to play
Over the hills and far away
Mommy duck said quack quack quack.
Two little ducks came running back.

Two little ducks went out to play
Over the hills and far away
Mommy duck said quack quack quack.
One little duck came running back.

One little duck went out to play
Over the hills and far away
Mommy duck said quack quack quack.
No little ducks came running back.

Then, Mommy looked around and
Mommy duck said loudly Quack Quack Quack,
Five little ducks came running back.

两 只 老 虎
兩 隻 老 虎
Liǎng zhī lǎo hǔ

Two Tigers

Two Tigers, two Tigers
Run so fast, run so fast.
One doesn't have ears,
One doesn't have a tail.
Isn't it strange? Isn't it strange?

两 只 老 虎，两 只 老 虎，
兩 隻 老 虎，兩 隻 老 虎，
Liǎng zhī lǎo hǔ, liǎng zhī lǎo hǔ,

跑 得 快，跑 得 快，
跑 得 快，跑 得 快，
pǎo dé kuài, pǎo dé kuài,

一 只 没 有 耳 朵，
一 隻 没 有 耳 朵，
Yì zhī méi yǒu ěr duō,

一 只 没 有 尾 巴，
一 隻 没 有 尾 巴，
yì zhī méi yǒu wěi bā,

真 奇 怪，真 奇 怪。
眞 奇 怪，眞 奇 怪。
zhēn qí guài, zhēn qí guài.

26

青 蛙 歌
青 蛙 歌

Qīng Wā Gē

一 只 青 蛙 一 张 嘴，
一 隻 青 蛙 一 張 嘴，
Yì zhī qīng wā yì zhāng zuǐ

两 个 眼 睛，四 条 腿。
兩 個 眼 睛，四 條 腿。
Liǎng gè yǎn jīng, sì tíao tuǐ.

扑 通 扑 通 跳 下 水，
撲 通 撲 通 跳 下 水，
Pū tōng pū tōng tiào xià shuǐ,

青 蛙 不 喝 水，真 奇 怪。
青 蛙 不 喝 水，眞 奇 怪。
Qīng wā bù hē shuǐ, zhēn qí guài.

青 蛙 不 喝 水，真 奇 怪。
青 蛙 不 喝 水，眞 奇 怪。
Qīng wā bù hē shuǐ, zhēn qí guài.

Frog Song

One frog, one mouth
Two eyes, four legs
"Splash, splash" jump in the water
The frog won't drink the water, how strange it is.
The frog won't drink the water, how strange it is.

打 雷，打 雷，
打 雷，打 雷
Dǎ léi, dǎ léi

打 雷，打 雷，
打 雷，打 雷，
Dǎ léi, dǎ léi,

声 音 大，声 音 大，
聲 音 大，聲 音 大，
Shēng yīn dà, shēng yīn dà,

淅 沥 哗 啦 下 雨，
淅 瀝 嘩 啦 下 雨，
Xī lì huā lā xià yǔ,

淅 沥 哗 啦 下 雨，
淅 瀝 嘩 啦 下 雨，
Xī lì huā lā xià yǔ,

我 湿 了，我 湿 了。
我 濕 了，我 濕 了。
Wǒ shī là, wō shī là.

There is Thunder

There is thunder, there is thunder
Hear it loud, hear it loud.
Pitter patter rain drops,
Pitter patter rain drops
I am wet, I am wet!

雨，雨，别 下 雨
雨，雨，别 下 雨
Yǔ, yǔ, bié xià yǔ

雨，雨，别 下 雨，以 后 再 下 雨。
雨，雨，别 下 雨，以 後 再 下 雨。
Yǔ, yǔ, bié xià yǔ yǐ hòu zài xià yǔ.

小＿＿ 要 玩 耍，雨，雨，别 下 雨。
小＿＿ 要 玩 耍，雨，雨，别 下 雨。
Xiǎo yào wán shuǎ, yǔ, yǔ, bié xià yǔ.

（一）汤 米 （二）潘 尼
（一）湯 米 （三）潘 尼
Tāng mǐ Pān ní

Rain, Rain, Go Away

Rain, rain, go away, come again another day
Little ＿＿ wants to play, rain, rain go away.
1) Tommy 2) Penny (Repeat)

小 星 星
小 星 星
Xiǎo xīng xīng

一 闪 一 闪 亮 晶 晶，
一 閃 一 閃 亮 晶 晶，
Yì shǎn yì shǎn liàng jīng jīng,

满 天 都 是 小 星 星，
滿 天 都 是 小 星 星，
mǎn tiān dōu shì xiǎo xīng xīng,

挂 在 天 上 放 光 明，
掛 在 天 上 放 光 明，
Guà zài tiān shàng fàng guāng míng,

好 像 许 多 小 眼 睛，
好 像 許 多 小 眼 睛，
hǎo xiàng xǔ duō xiǎo yǎn jīng,

一 闪 一 闪 亮 晶 晶，
一 閃 一 閃 亮 晶 晶，
Yì shǎn yì shǎn liàng jīng jīng,

满 天 都 是 小 星 星。
滿 天 都 是 小 星 星。
mǎn tiān dōu shì xiǎo xīng xīng.

Little Stars

Twinkle, twinkle bright little star,
The whole sky full of little stars,
Up above the sky, like many many small eyes.
Twinkle, twinkle bright star,
The whole sky full of small stars.

再　　见
再　　見
Zài　jiàn

你　好，你　好，
你　好，你　好，
Nǐ　hǎo,　nǐ　hǎo,

我　很　好，我　很　好。
我　很　好，我　很　好。
Wǒ　hén　hǎo,　wǒ　hén　hǎo.

唱　歌　真　快　乐，
唱　歌　眞　快　樂，
Chàng gē　zhēn kuài lè,

唱　歌　真　快　乐，
唱　歌　眞　快　樂，
Chàng gē　zhēn kuài lè,

再　见，再　见。
再　見，再　見。
Zài　jiàn,　Zài　jiàn.

Good-bye

How are you? How are you?
I am fine. I am fine.
Singing is fun, Singing is fun.
Good-bye. Good-bye

GREETINGS

Hello	nǐ hǎo
Good-bye	zàijiàn
My name is __	Wǒ jiào __
Thank you	xièxie
You're welcome.	bú kèqì

FAMILY & FRIENDS

baby	wáwa
mother	māma
father	bàba
grandmother	nǎinai
grandfather	yéye
older sister	jiějie
little sister	mèimei
older brother	gēge
little brother	dìdi
friend	péngyǒu

ANIMALS

bees	mìfēng
bird	niǎo
cat	māo
chicken	jī
cow	niú
dog	gǒu
ducks	yā
frog	qīngwā
lamb	xiǎoyáng
panda	xióngmāo
pig	zhū
tiger	hǔ

COLORS

black	hēi
blue	lán
brown	zōng
green	lǜ
orange	júhuáng
pink	fěnhóng
purple	zǐ
red	hóng
white	bái
yellow	huáng

NATURE

cloud	yún
flowers	huā
garden	yuán
hill	xiǎoshān
moon	yuè
night	yèwǎn
pond	chítáng
rain	yǔ
rainbow	cǎihóng
sky	tiān
snow	xuě
star	xīng
sun	tàiyáng
thunder	léi
water	shuǐ

ACTIONS

brush teeth	shuā yá
clap	pāipai shǒu
comb hair	shū tóu
drink	hē
fall	dǎoxià
hooray	wànsuì
jump	tiào
laugh	xiào
run	pǎobù
sing	chàng
sleep	shuìjiào
wash face	xǐ liǎn

BODY PARTS

ears	ěrduo
eyes	yǎnjīng
face	liǎn
feet	jiǎo
fingers	shǒuzhǐ
hair	tóufa
hands	shǒu
head	tóu
knees	xī
mouth	kǒu, zuǐbā
nose	bízǐ
shoulders	jiānbǎng

THINGS

balloons	qìqiú
bridge	qíao
car	qìchē
clothes	yīfú
cup	bēi
home	jiā
house	fángzǐ
doll	yángwáwa
paint	túliào
pants	kùzǐ
pencil	qiānbǐ
shirt	chènshān
shoes	xié

NUMBERS

one	yī
two	èr
three	sān
four	sì
five	wǔ
six	liù
seven	qī
eight	bā
nine	jiǔ
ten	shí
eleven	shíyī
twenty	èrshí
100	yìbǎi

ADJECTIVES

big	dà
happy	xìng
left	zuǒ
long	cháng
loud	dà shēng
right	yòu
small	xiǎo
wet	shī

SEASONS

spring	chūnjì
summer	xiàjì
fall	qiūjì
winter	dōngjì

1. How are You? *Page 4*

Have one child sing the beginning part of the song and the others do the second part. Replace the word "sing" with any other action words such as dance or jump.

2. Ten Little Friends *Page 5*

Helps with counting. Point at the illustration or place paper/flannel dolls one at a time as you count friends.

3. This is the Way We Wash Our Face *Page 6*

This is a popular song in Chinese. Children could act out what they are singing. The repetitive patterns in this song help children learn the song .

4. When We are Together *Page 8*

Popular song. Ask children who they like to be with and who makes them happy.

5. If You are Happy *Page 10*

This popular song enhances young children's listening skills by following the directions in the song. Replace the movement with other actions.

6. Little Working Bees *Page 12*

This is a very popular Chinese children's song. Replace "Buzz" sound and bees with other animals and their sounds.

7. London Big Bridge *Page 13*

You can act out the song like the illustration. Two children can join hands and form an arch. The other children form a single line to pass under the bridge. When the bridge falls at the end of the song, the child who is under the bridge becomes one of the children holding hands to make the arch.

8. Sing a Song and Dance *Page 14*

This great sing-and-play song helps children become familiar with body parts in Chinese. Also teaches the concept of "in" and "out". Follow the action of the words.

9. Head, Shoulders, Knees & Feet *Page 16*

Great for gross motor skill development while learning about body parts in Chinese. Follow the song by pointing at the head, shoulders, knees & feet with both hands.

10. Two Ears *Page 17*

Excellent for helping children remember the body parts. Ask children to fill in the numbers. For example, the teacher or parent sings "ears" and children say "2". Follow the song by pointing at the body parts with both hands. When it comes to the ten fingers, move all ten fingers. Clap hands as you sing "la, la, la ....".

11. Little Sister Had a Little Lamb *Page 18*

Replace "little sister" with any children's name.

12. Where is My Friend? *Page 19*

Play a hide-and-seek game with this song. Practice learning family members by replacing "friend" with "daddy," "mommy," "brother," or "sister".

13. Doll in the Garden *Page 20*

The word "little sister" in Chinese is used generically to refer to little girls in Chinese.

14. What Color? *Page 21*

This song helps children learn names of different colors. You can use the cover of the book for the color of clothes and rainbows. Red is a very lucky color in Chinese culture. Chinese like to wear red on Chinese New Year's Day, at weddings, and at birthday parties.

15. Old Mr. Wong has a Farm Field *Page 22*

"Wong" is a very common Chinese name. In China, most farmers do not have farms they have fields. This song introduces animals and their sounds in Chinese to children.

16. Five Little Ducks *Page 24*

You can use flannel ducks or duck puppets made out of paper and glued to popsicle sticks to act out the song.

17. Two Tigers *Page 26*

This is one of the most popular Chinese children's songs. Ask children to move as if they were a tiger. Ask children what will happen to the tiger if it doesn't have ears or eyes, or tail.

18. Frog Song *Page 27*

This popular Chinese song is excellent for teaching math. Ask if two or three frogs jumped into the water, how many eyes, legs would there be in total.

19. There is Thunder *Page 28*

Ask children what the sound of thunder is like. Put cupped hands next to the ears as the second verse is sung and move fingers to simulate rain as arms are lowered.

20. Rain, Rain, Go Away *Page 28*

Use different children's names to help children become familiar with each other's name. Ask children about what they can do in a rainy day.

21. Little Star *Page 29*

Popular song. Use finger movement to simulate the twinkles.

22. Good-Bye *Page 30*

"Good-bye" in Chinese literally means "See you again."